TIMOTHY, MY PROMISE TO YOU IN THE NEXT 50 YEARS...

TIMOTHY, MY PROMISE TO YOU IN THE NEXT 50 YEARS...

MORGAN PLANTZ

Baugh

Made Baugh Us

Contents

I   I

I

Timothy,
My Promise to You, in the next 50 years...

There Will Come a Day

There will come a day when good things and bad things happen. I'm crazy, I'm insane, I'm funny, and I can be depressing. I will make you want to quit but I can make you want to stay, hopefully. I've always been this way. But in the next 50 years, I promise I will try to change my bad habits and the things you strongly dislike about me and the things I know for a fact are a pain. A relationship involves a *lot* of love, a *lot* of patience, and a *whole lot* of forgiveness. Stick with me until the day we die and I promise there will be more good days than bad.

Aristotle said, "love is composed of one soul inhabiting two bodies". I believe we have one soul together, and we each got half of a whole. We must work together to make it one. That is easier said than done, and it may take a lifetime but I know it will all work out in the end. As you read the following pages of this book I have written you, I will take you into the past but I will also take you into the future. While the present may be hard, it will be worth it.

Chapter 1
When We are Hot and Lean

There will come a day when we are able to lose the weight we have gained. Your muscles will tighten all over again, and my breasts will perk up like they did before I had kids. My booty will be bubbly and round, and your abs will show, just as they did in the Marine Corps. We will exercise together when the kids get older. When we finally have time to take care of ourselves after years of blood, sweat, and tears being put into raising these four little souls.

Where we were once so attractive, but we fell into the groove of family, life, and stress, that it took the largest piece of our self-esteem away. I am afraid to show my body now because of the toll of birthing children. You hate looking in the mirror because you think you look like an ogre. But just remember, weight can be lost. Muscles can be gained. Maybe not now or in the near future. One day for sure, we will get back to our titillating selves.

Think of all the marvelous meals we have convened together as a family at and gorged ourselves with. The roasts, the alfredo, the rice, the soups, and don't forget the creamy chicken noodles and mashed potatoes. The goulash and the spaghetti too. Together in the kitchen, cooking those meals as a team of two. No matter if we were fighting, we were stars in the kitchen as a duo. No matter how broke we were, we always got fed and the babies *always* had full bellies.

For now, we just love each other for who we are not what our bodies *used* to look like. We can look toward the future when we have the time and space to exercise with grace. We have our memories in photos that we can look forward to in the approaching years.

Love isn't defined as what a person looks like on the outside. Love is a feeling. Looks change, and muscles fade. At the end of the day, we have our memories of a life we made. So stop worrying about what we perceive ourselves like now compared to when we started dating. That was a lifetime ago. We will get back there one day. In time.

We get to remember the times when you couldn't put your socks on because your very full belly from dinner prevented you from bending over. You thought you were fat, but in those very few moments, you got to stop taking care of everyone else, and I got to take care of you. And the times when I would get stuck on top of a chair and not be able to get down, and you would turn around and have me grab onto your shoulders. I was heavy but you still did it and we would laugh that I slinked down your back so I didn't break it. Moments in time that will not be forgotten. A laugh holds a place in a specific neuron in the brain. What memory would have taken the place of that one?

Don't give up just because our bodies don't look like we want them to. How dumb would it be to ruin a millennium just because I got a little chubby? Or because your belly looks like you're 7 months pregnant? How trivial. Buck up, we will be chubby and happy together until the day when we are thinner and more flexible collectively. I promise you I will try.

TIMOTHY, MY PROMISE TO YOU IN THE NEXT 50 YEARS…
~ 5

Chapter 2
When We are Old and Gray

There will come a day when we are hot and lean but also a day when we are old and gray. Our skin will sag in areas, when we were younger, that we said would never happen to us. We were immature and sexy. Our stomachs were tight and flat. Our muscles were strong and we had six packs. We could bike for miles and run for hours.

We would take a thousand photos of ourselves, clothed and naked. We would show off to others because of the attention our bodies brought. We never even thought of the consequences of who saw us, but now we are worried and scared for anyone to recognize us. We will think we are despicable because we have not aged very gracefully. Gray and white will shine through where our beautiful brown and black hair once flowed.

We may gain weight in every corner of our bodies. No matter what we try, we can't get rid of it. Our belly might get big and round and our booties will flatten. My breast will sag more and your balls will hang lower. Your muscles will fall and I will have wrinkles all over. When we once sat and watched television together over the years and commented on how much our favorite actors aged, we will be the actors aging in our real life.

Our minds will fade, and we may not remember a whole lot of things. It'll start with small instances and may happen more often. We will get annoyed with each other forgetting the most important things. The outer cortex of our brain will slowly degenerate. We will be slower at responding, but don't assume the other is ignoring us. All we can do is take as many photos as we can, and videos that make our hearts happy. We can look through our albums and remember the good times, even if all we know at that time is what we see in that 4x6 inch square.

Growing old isn't a bad concept. It means we have lived for more years together. Raised a family for many more. We've learned, we've grown, and we've made mistakes. But most importantly, we have survived. And we have survived together. We've raised our children to the best of our ability and hope they will have come out of it as respectful, loving, independent adults. They will have children that we can give advice to them about, and tell them all of the things we did not so right, so that they may not make the same mistakes we did twice.

Throughout the years, and many ups and downs, one day we will be sitting on our wrap-around porch, sipping on some whiskey, and one of us may look at the other, and notice that what we looked like never really mattered. The way we loved more than we hated each other, the way we kissed more than we grimaced, the way we laughed and hugged more than we argued and fought. That is what really meant the most.

Chapter 3
When we have all of the Money in the World

There will come a day when we have all of the money in the world. When we can go out and not worry about how much a gallon of milk is, or get that new fancy gaming computer that you can play your old Windows 95 games on and not have to worry about an old beat-up tower's motherboard going out. Where we can buy each kid their own laptop and every electronic device they have their eyes on that year.

A day where out of the blue, you can come home from your run on the road and say grab your to-go bags, we are going on a trip. And we will load up the car with the kids and travel to all of the places we talked about visiting. We would go to your old stomping grounds in South Carolina, and we will go to Niagara Falls as a family, even though you have already been. We will go see the Redwood Forest, just for a time, and get out of California as fast as we can. Hit the road, and drive to Colorado to see the beautiful landscape of the Southern Rockies. We will hike through the Adirondacks, and swim with the sharks in Florida.

Even without money, we have captured pictures of so many covered bridges. When we have the money, we can go see even more. And what we know of being less than blue collar, we will save some more so that our children can go to college or a trade school and have a better life than we did when we were poor. And we can look towards the future of maybe living in Italy and raising the kids abroad. We can do anything we want to. Maybe just stay in the beautiful home we have now and make it more. Anything we do, we will be overjoyed, I know.

I think the most important thing to look forward to is being financially stable and not having to stress over the bills. Traveling and spending is insignificant, but being able to thrive in another recession, just as we had in 2019 through 2022 with the recession and poor management of our government made the smallest of necessities so expensive that even the most common folk couldn't afford them. We will have a stockpile big enough to sustain us for a few years, and not have to travel to the grocery store every week just for the simplest of things. We will get there, we just have to hold on. I can't promise it will be easy to get to this point, but I promise we will be happy no matter where we end up.

TIMOTHY, MY PROMISE TO YOU IN THE NEXT 50 YEARS...
~ 11

Chapter 4
When We are Worth a Paltry Penny

There will come a day when we are richer than rich, but there will also come a day when we are only worth a paltry penny. When we have no money and are looking for pennies in our cushions. When we are worth less than a piece of trash on the side of a street. Every couple goes through hard times financially. One day we have money, the next we have empty pockets. Days harder than that of the Covid-19 era.

We scraped by but always managed to get our bills paid, and kept the kids' bellies so full. Our worst years were during this time. The stress of leaving a job that paid so much, but treated you like garbage. To go from buying whatever we wanted, to saving up just so our kids had good birthday gifts. You worried, stressed, cried, and got pissed. I tried what I could to help take off some heaviness. But each day we woke up, we had a roof over our heads. The kids were fed. Our lights were on. All of the worries slowly went away.

With 50 years ahead of us, we will more than likely fall into that era again. Whether it be soon or later, it may or may not happen. But if it does, we will know one thing. We stuck together, side by side, and made what little money we could manage to find. Look toward the future, look forward to a happier life. Don't lose your hope like you very often do in times of duress. With six people depending on you, four of which are small little hearts, I know it must be very hard. One day when they are older, they will get to hear the stories of how Daddy worked his butt off to keep our family afloat.

Going through these hard times can toughen our hearts

and minds. To know that one day we can have money, and the next we can have zero. We will no longer take advantage of a few hundred bills. We will tuck it in our envelopes and hide it for another rainy day. This time will teach us a lesson that will make us as a family grow. We just need to remember, it is us six against the world, not us against each other.

We came into your life like a wrecking ball. One day you were young and single and rich and the next you were a Dad of four. You gave us things we never had before. You're doing a great job no matter what you think when you are gone. My promise is to try to be an easier partner in these hardest of times. And to be more frugal and not so spoiled. It might take me a while to figure it out, but I promise to try.

Chapter 5
When we are so in Love

There will come a day when we are so in love it is intoxicating. Where we can't look away from the other because we will be afraid the moment will end. We will sit by each other and watch our cheesy Christmas movies and "ooh" and "aww" at the way we feel the same as the fake romances on t.v. I'll be doing dishes and you will come by and smack me on the butt and I will turn around and smirk at your adorableness.

You'll tell me good morning darlin' like you did the morning after we met, and I will tell you good morning my love and we will slowly embrace. The passion behind your kisses, and the way you tell me you love my crinkly nose will be all that matters at that moment. And then our kids will come stomping into the room and take over our king-sized bed as they do. And we will lay altogether and waste away the day.

We will take our family pictures every year so we can reminisce about the way we loved one another. To see our happy, smiling faces still on a piece of paper that will outlast our life. We will see the way we changed, the good and the bad, and notice the way we have grown as a family and as a couple. I love the way you are so excited for that time of year instead of dreading it. We will match and smile and laugh. And we will print them off and add them to our walls of love.

You'll lay your head on my lap so I can run my hands through your hair. One of your love languages. My fingers will travel down your forehead and rub your temples and glide across your brow. And then I will rub down your sideburns into your beautiful beard and back up around your ears. That is the way we cuddle each other.

We will spend all of our time together as we do now. It's not everyone's cup of tea but when you are each other's best and, only friends, and the love of each other's lives, it isn't an issue. That's the way we love our hermit life together. Where we can sit and homeschool the kids together and spend even more time together and as a family. We will go on walks and talk about the trees, and the architecture of houses. Tell the kids stories of our pasts as we are strolling down the sidewalks.

We will work together on our yearly garden. I pull you till. We will sow our seeds in the garden and in love and watch both of them grow. We will bicker at the other on the hottest of days to see who has to go water the garden and sweat their booties off. And we will end up both out there watering just for you to be able to spray me with the hose like you always have done. And we will laugh and act like two kids in the sun. At the end of the growing season, we will reap what we have sown and feed our children our labors of love. As a family, we will make salsa and taste each batch and go through five bags of tortilla chips at the same time because it is so delightful.

TIMOTHY, MY PROMISE TO YOU IN THE NEXT 50 YEARS...

17

Chapter 6
When We Dislike Each Other's Guts

There will come a day we love each other so much, but there will also come a day when we hate each other's guts. Every couple has them, and we have probably had more than we should. Whether it stems from money troubles caused by the government and its evil ways of inflation, or by things that we annoy each other with, those days will come. We can either learn from them or let them affect our relationship so negatively that there is no way of going back.

I am an annoying person. I have always been told this. I get stressed easily, and anxious over nothing constantly. I hate taking out the trash and always forget when it is the actual trash day, so I don't remind you half the time. I am all over the place all the time. I don't know how to do some simple tasks and it will irritate the crap out of you. It takes me hours to do the dishes and then my body hurts for hours more after. We have four children which means the house is normally chaotic and hard to keep up with cleaning up all of the time. I suck at laundry so some days it piles too high.

I stay at home to teach the kids and to keep up on housework as much as I can but some days I am so exhausted just from waking up that sometimes things don't get done but surviving. You won't understand and will get irritated. I have so many flaws and annoying habits.

You chew with your mouth open and are the loudest eater. It is so incredibly eye-twitching to hear. You are a hothead and get mad very quickly at sometimes the smallest of things. And we will both be irritated at each other and it turns into an argument. We are both terrible at saying sorry and forgetting about our grudges. Some days we will not want anything to do with each other but we always want to be in the same house if not the same room as one another. This way we can stew and glare but still be spending time together. Because no matter what we are mad at each other about, we still love even when we struggle to like each other.

If I wake up too early and haven't had my coffee, I am quick to get pissy. I don't mean to do it but that's how my brain is. And when it is that time of the month, I will be on an emotional roller coaster for two weeks and it'll seem like it is never going to end. But you have to remember it is a health problem not a mental problem like you think most of the time. I am almost over 30 now so it won't be much longer, hold on.

My promise to you in the next 50 years is that even when we hate each other, we will try our absolute best to forgive and forget and move on with our day. We might not be very good about that now but within the next 50, we will definitely get our quarrels and qualms figured out. I promise we will conquer any fight we will ever have, me and you, together.

Chapter 7
When We Laugh Uncontrollably

There will come a day when we laugh uncontrollably. Where every little thing gets a chuckle or a belly laugh out of the other. From just the way you look in the morning to the weird and funny faces, we make at each other. Even just making eye contact will make us giggle. These are the moments we will live for. The goofy ways the kids have of doing simple things to the ridiculously random things they come up with.

You will reenact the funniest of impressions. From your weird voices to your goofy faces. We will be awake at 2 a.m. getting ready to send you off to work, and we will spend the whole time talking in all kinds of accents for no reason. You'll laugh at the childlike ways I take criticism because you think it is so cute, and I will laugh at the way you get so heated when talking about politics because I think it is so ridiculous.

You tickle me and bust a gut due to the crazy sounds that come out of my mouth. From the monkey laugh to the hyena, and the dolphin sounds in between. And it will make me laugh even harder because your laugh is hilarious too. When we are out in public and can look at each other and know what the other is thinking, that will bring a giggle and a high five. We really are two peas in a pod. There is an anonymous person that once said " The goal is to laugh forever with the person you take seriously" and I can't think of a more truthful statement.

We will go out on dates and dress up in matching hats and laugh at the looks and conversations others are having about us. We will have a few drinks and be funny together and laugh at the others saying we are crazy. We are crazy but we are crazy in love and life. My promise to you is that there will be more laughter than none in the next 50 years...

TIMOTHY, MY PROMISE TO YOU IN THE NEXT 50 YEARS...

Chapter 8
When We Don't Speak At All

There will come a day when all we do is laugh, but there will also come a day when we don't speak at all. It's a hard fact of life that no matter how much someone loves another, there will be days when we struggle to even have a conversation. Whether it be from an argument, or when one of us dreams of the other doing something stupid, in these times we are bad at not speaking to the other for some time. I know I am worse at this than you are but we equally can work together to talk it out.

Our communication is not up to par as it should be and I would much rather go in another room and stew for a while, while you want to keep the argument going so you can get your point across. These are both bad habits of ours. One day we may focus more on the hurt of the past than on the beauties of the future. While a lot of the problems stem from me and my crazy ways, you are also at fault for some situations. We need to take the blame for our own actions and give the other credit where credit is due. I know one day we will be able to get this communication thing under control, especially when we literally talk all day long.

This is a very hard chapter to dwell over because I know we have had a lot of arguments over me not wanting to talk about stuff. When I do want to talk it is right before we go to sleep and you have to go to work a few hours more. So then we end up arguing over switching places about who wanted to communicate at that time and why they couldn't speak at the time the other was ready. It is a vicious cycle that I for sure need to work on. My promise to you is that there is always the next day and we need to apologize more than we are quiet. I will do my best to talk more when you are ready, even if it makes my anxiety swelter. I love you more than a stupid squabble.

Chapter 9
When We Are So Thankful We Stuck Together

There will come a day when we are so thankful we stuck together all of these years. Through many, many tough times, feuds, and emotions, we will be able to look back on them and be grateful we always made up. Forgiving my stupidity and forgiving your anger, paved the way for a lifetime of much better days. I was bad about saying I am just going to leave, but all I wanted you to do was ask me to stay. I was stubborn (and still am), and you were the most uncaring, caring person that I ever met (and still am).

We will sit together on our porch and drink our coffee and look out at our kids playing, and hopefully their kids also. We will grab the other's hand and look into each other's eyes and smile a smile that is strong enough to feel deep down into our hearts. We will tell stories of our love and teach our growing children what to do and what not to do in a relationship to keep it happy and healthy, although we will probably still be trying to figure that out completely.

There have been instances that we have been close to breaking up a hundred times but there were a million times more that we were so happy together. To focus on these instances more than the bad is the road to having a long, loving, life together. In the next 50 years, we will be vacationing as a whole and will have fewer fights and disagreements, and we will call the other out when they are getting too heated. We will remind each one to be calm towards the other and remember it's us v.s. the world not you v.s. Me and vice versa.

I will love you
As long as the sun
Burns in the sky,
As long as the moon
Shines its light
Into the dark night,
Until the raging
Blue oceans become
Calm and dry.
I will love you
Until the end of time.

~Christy Ann Martine~

I promise I will love you until the end of time...

TIMOTHY, MY PROMISE TO YOU IN THE NEXT 50 YEARS...

Chapter 10
All This Time Was a Waste

There will come a day when we are so thankful we stayed, but there will also come a day when we think all this time was a waste. When all of our petty arguments and fights about idiotic stuff are so often and so overwhelming that all we want to do is up and leave. When the other's actions are so annoying that it feels that it is not even worth having the bad day that will ensue.

Our previous quarrels ended in you going to work early or me leaving with the kids for a few hours or overnight. Too bad we couldn't just decide to leave the argument instead of the house. So many wasted minutes and days that were spent feuding and being mad at each other, when we could have been snuggling and making up to one another. The difficult times during the holidays when I struggled to find love because of my past. I took it out on you and ruined many days.

I would prefer this chapter to be a waste because for us to move forward we must forget all these petty fights we have had. Let's look to tomorrow or the next minute and decide to love instead of hate. I forgive you, you forgive me, let's not have to think that leaving is okay. I will leave you with my promise to you in the next 50 years, to never again say the words "I am leaving you" again. From this day on we deal with our crap and move on together. That's my promise to you. And I am sorry for all of the arguments I have caused.

TIMOTHY, MY PROMISE TO YOU IN THE NEXT 50 YEARS…

Chapter 11
When We Get Married

We have been together for years, and are still unwed. Whether it be because we aren't getting along that day or because you don't think the financial situation is the best. But this one thing is true, I will one day be wedded to you. You placed a ring on my finger that you designed just for me and told me you promised to marry me one day. Then you joked and gave me a signed paper with a date that we would be wed by. It took me a while to realize that that day in February doesn't exist but you thought it funny anyway.

One day you will see that money shouldn't have made it so we hadn't wed sooner. That all one needs in a marriage is love. I will love you in wealth and love you in poverty. I want to be able to see our Golden Anniversary and sit in the chairs for the county fair's photograph of the people who have been married for 50 years and more, and we will be in the paper as one of the ones that made it. Our kids will look towards their future because they get to see their parents so in love for so many years.

I will have your last name as will the kids and we will be the official Baughs of the sea. We already decorate our walls in Bs and you call me Momma Baugh and the kids already use your last name for all of their schoolwork. That little piece of paper may not mean much to you, but to the world, we are nothing but a boyfriend and girlfriend and I want them to be way more. I want to dress in a beautiful olive green gown and have the boys walk me down the aisle, while the girls are ahead throwing flower petals all around. We will have Grandpa dressed as a cowboy telling us to repeat our vows.

It doesn't have to be huge and glamorous and we probably won't have anyone watching, but our family of six because those are who matter the most. We will sit together and make our decorations with our hands and the kids, and we will have the wedding we want to have and not try to impress anyone.

We may not have a perfect and easy life but I promise no matter what we go through we will do it as one. I will care for you when you are ill and make sure your belly is always fed with good food. We will slowly but surely get to live out our dreams. You, and me, and our four little Bs. I hope you'll end up taking the chance with me.

Chapter 12
When We are on our Deathbed

There will come a day when we are on our deathbeds and we will reminisce about every day we laughed together and had fun. I will hold your hand and you will hold mine, and we will tell the tales that we remember the best. We will talk about our first night together and cry about how this might be our last. I wish I could have met you sooner so I could have loved you longer. But somehow our love story, through the ups and the very downs, was the precursor to a very tremendous thing.

I will always believe that we were destined to be. From all of my tattoos, I had previous to knowing you matching up with everything about you, to meeting you for the first time and we both acknowledged we knew each other and just couldn't figure out why. I believe in the red thread of fate. I knew I would find you one day though I didn't know how long it would take and how much pain we both had to go through in order to find the end of the line.

The red thread of fate is when two people are connected by an imaginary red thread, regardless of time, place, or circumstance, wrapped around their ring fingers. This is the finger that has the biggest vessel to the heart. That thread may stretch and tangle but it will *never* break. Our threads definitely stretched and tangled for a very long time, but now our thread ends are right beside each other.

There will come a day. And then another. And another. No matter what we do, whether it is loving or hating each other. We will always have another day together. Until death do we part. May we focus on everything good we have been given and work on being a little less fickle. Love more than fighting. Kiss more than arguing. A little less crazy (me) and a little more patient. More forgiving and fewer grudges held. I will end this book with this:

"There will always come a day. Let's always have another day together. Invariably and without fail. I profess to you, my love engraved on these pages forever so that the whole world will know that I loved you then, I love you now, and I will love you for eternity. I love you, my best friend, my confidant, my Loopy."

TIMOTHY, MY PROMISE TO YOU IN THE NEXT 50 YEARS...

www.ingramcontent.com/pod-product-compliance
Lightning Source LLC
Chambersburg PA
CBHW040741060526
44119CB00074B/186